DEMOCRACY TODAY IN RUSSIA

HAROLD E. ROGERS, JR.

AuthorHouse™
1663 Liberty Drive, Suite 200
Bloomington, IN 47403
www.authorhouse.com
Phone: 1-800-839-8640

© 2009 Harold E. Rogers, Jr.. All rights reserved.

No part of this book may be reproduced, stored in a retrieval system, or transmitted by any means without the written permission of the author.

First published by AuthorHouse 4/7/2009

ISBN: 978-1-4389-6937-4 (sc)

Printed in the United States of America
Bloomington, Indiana

This book is printed on acid-free paper.

ABOUT THIS BOOK

DEMOCRACY TODAY IN RUSSIA

This Book, **Democracy Today in Russia**, becomes available at an opportune time. Far reaching political and economic changes are occurring throughout the world as are the leaders who will bring them about. On January 20, 2009 Barak Obama was sworn in as President of the United States. He replaces George W. Bush whose policies toward the world, including Russia, were becoming increasingly counter productive. Leadership in Russia has undergone significant changes within the past year. Russia is now led by a young team, Vladimir Putin former President and now Prime Minister and Dmitri Medvedev now President, hand picked by Putin . These leaders contend that they are achieving Democracy in Russia. Western scholars are not so sure. President Obama will have to test the new Russia and do his best to make Russia a more reliable partner in solving the multitude of challenges both countries face.

Communism collapsed in Russia in December, 1991 and was replaced by a rambunctious democracy overseen by Boris Yeltsin.

Historic Church in Moscow on Red Square

New Moscow cathedral

U. S General Colin Powell

Last president of the USSR, Mikhail Gorbachev

Yeltsin achieved a great deal as a wrecker of the old order, but lacked the temperament and good health to bring about a successful economy and workable democracy demanded by Russian citizens. Since becoming president of Russia through appointment, Vladimir Putin has brought order out of chaos and prosperity for increasing numbers out of penury. This book explores the steps Putin and Medvedev have taken to reach this mark in the Russian journey toward peace and prosperity; and whether and to what extent they have sacrificed democracy along the way. Perhaps there is no direct path from Russia in its present state to the Russia of peace and prosperity.

Russian soldiers in Stalingrad

Winter in Stalingrad

Tanks in Moscow, after revolution

The author has reviewed new and developing ideas floated by the Russian leaders to mark their proposed path forward. Putin wants to make Russia a modern country and in doing so provide a successful fight against crime and corruption. He and Medvedev, both of whom are graduate lawyers, say they want to strengthen the rule of law. Putin also is seeking acceptance of a new political concept called sovereign democracy which is a form approved by a country's own internal electorate, but not necessarily by any other country. They want to continue to wrest control of national assets from the oligarchs which they propose to operate for the benefit of the nation as a whole under a system called State Capitalism.

Many of the objectives sought by Putin and Medvedev sound a lot like communism and a command economy. This book will discuss the significance of these totalitarian detours from the road toward democracy.

About the Author

The author, Harold E. Rogers, Jr. earned both history (1952) and law (1955) degrees at Stanford University, graduating Phi Beta Kappa. Following military service in Italy as a first lieutenant in the Army JAGC, Mr. Rogers organized a law firm in San Francisco specializing in public finance and litigation. He thereafter founded regional finance practices for two nationally recognized law firms. In the meantime he continued his career in writing which he had begun with a publication in the Stanford Law Review. This was followed by articles published on a wide variety of subjects, including volumes on California water history, and development in Russia and China. Mr. Rogers was a lecturer at the Stanford Law and Business schools where he developed and delivered a semester course entitled "Problems of Doing Business in Russia and the CIS". He has been a member of San Francisco Trade delegations to both China and Russia. He learned something of the practical side of American politics in supporting the election campaigns of President Jimmy Carter. Carter appointed Mr. Rogers chairman of the Commission on the Review of the Federal Impact Aid Program

Since publication in 2007 of The History of Democracy from the Middle East to Western Civilization in both English and Russian, Mr. Rogers has written for publication in 2009 a volume entitled Democracy Today in Russia.

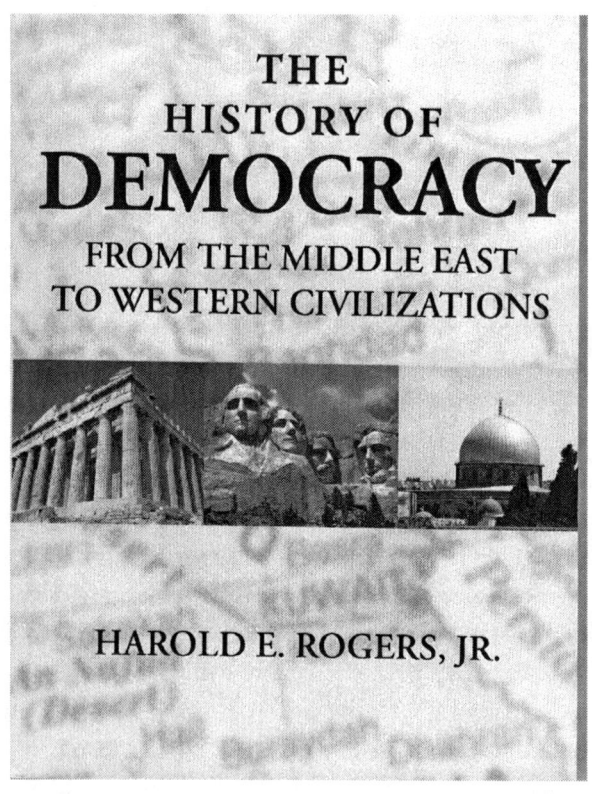

Cover of History of Democracy

DEMOCRACY TODAY IN RUSSIA

TABLE OF CONTENTS

Introduction 1
Putin's Plan to Make Russia into a Modern Country ... 7
Putin's background and qualifications for Presidency . 17
    Putin's Prompt Actions after Appointment as
        President 19
    Putin's Personal Finances 20
    Putin's Agenda 21
        Fight Corruption 22
        Strengthen rule of law 22
        Further Sovereign Democracy 23
        Adopt Democratic Procedures 23
        Carry Out Kyoto Protocol by cleaning
            environment 23
        Negotiate for Multipolar world 23
        Complete negotiations for military
            security of borders 24
        Fight national epidemics of AIDS and
            alcoholism 24
        Control Oligarchs and recover State
            Property 24
        Strengthen internal power 24
        Strengthen State Capitalism and financial
            power 25
        Rebuild State infrastructure for transport,
            schools and public buildings 25

- Increase social benefits for medical services, pension and related benefits 25
- Organized Crime and Corruption and other matters for the Russian Agenda 27
- Criticism Of Nemtsov, Milov And Others 34
- Russian History and Culture which will guide Putin . 41
  - Joseph Stalin 42
  - Nikita Sergeyevich Khrushchev 47
  - Leonid Brezhnev 49
  - Yuri Vladimirovich Andropov 54
  - Konstantin Ustinovich Chernenko 55
  - Mikhail Sergeyevich Gorbachev 56
  - Boris Nikolayevich Yeltsin 61
- Who started the South Ossetia, Georgia war 71
- Conclusion 85

DEMOCRACY TODAY IN RUSSIA

INTRODUCTION

"The Russian people, Dostoyevsky once said, believe so fervently in an all powerful czar that this ideal is bound to influence the whole future course of our history." [1] Russia appears to have adopted an imitation of democracy. It is as if a veneer of legitimacy has been put on a variation of the strongman rule present in Russia for centuries whether under Peter the Great, Lenin or Putin.

A parliamentary election was held in December, 2007 in which many parties took part, but only United Russia (Mr. Vladimir Putin's party) received glowing television news coverage and other government favors; it won in a landslide. Dmitri A. Medvedev, Putin's aide was endorsed as the Presidential candidate and was assured of winning in March, 2008. However a day after Medvedev was endorsed, he announced that he wanted Putin to be his prime minister and thus Putin was able to keep substantial power even though he gave up the Presidency. Why did Putin go through the motions of a legitimate election? He could without doubt have persuaded the

---

[1] NY Times, Dec. 16, 2007.

electorate to extend his term as President. In fact, legislation has now been introduced allowing the constitution to extend the presidential term. Putin appears in part to be motivated to need to be seen on the world stage, not simply as a dictator but rather a lawful popular representative of the Russian people.

Russians have shown no great hunger for Western style democracy. Polls confirm that there would be little dissent if Putin stayed on as president for another term. The Kremlin dominates television and has cracked down on the opposition. However a diversity of voices flourish in newspapers where criticism of Putin is not uncommon. Similarly criticism is found on the internet. Mikhail Khordorkovsky, an arch foe of Putin, is presently serving a jail sentence for fraud, but writes from his prison cell that "Putin certainly is no liberal and no democrat, but nontheless, he is more liberal and democratic than 70 percent of the population of our country."[2] Especially after the turmoil of the post communist years Russians have a tendency to be drawn to a strong leader. They crave stability, consumer goods and travel—things that were denied before.

Political structures in Russia are still developing. The rule of law is shaky and people in power do not have accountability. Thus the government is shaped by the

---

[2] See Wikipedia, Putin, p. 5; The continuation of Khordorkovsky's (President of Yukos) criminal prosecution attaches to the public perception in Russia that the oligarchs are thieves who unjustly enriched themselves by robbing the country of its natural wealth. This (the Yukos Affair) marked a turning point in Russia's commitment to domestic property rights and the rule of law.

leaders' instincts about what the people expect and will bear.[3] Following Putin's statement of his future plans to remain in power as Medvedev's prime minister, President Bush and the US executive branch appeared to accept his decision without any formal or informal objection, feeling there was not much they could do to change the Kremlin's position.[4]

Bit by bit Russia has chipped away at whatever democratic structure it possessed, following adoption of Yeltsin's constitution. Among other actions President Putin has

a) weakened checks and balances within the state,

b) diminished political and legal transparency, and

c) made it impossible for independent media, political parties and nongovernmental groups to flourish.

Bush's National Security Strategy acknowledged that in Russia "recent trends regrettably point toward a diminishing commitment to democratic freedoms and institutions." Although running out of time, Bush said he had not given up on Russia. Unfortunately an increasingly authoritarian Russia, is less likely to work in concert with the West. Some evidence in this regard: Putin has supported the fraudulent reelection of Alexander Lukashenko of Belarus, one of the last dictators in Europe.

---

3   Ibid.
4   See Washington Post, Oct 5, 2007.

Similarly Putin has opposed democratic candidates in Georgia and Ukraine.[5]

Putin's goal is to make Russia a modern country. He is brutally honest in public about how backward Russia is and has definite ideas about how to achieve his goals. Russian GNP should, he expects, be doubled in 10 years. This will provide the financial underpinning to make Russia look more like a European country. Putin intends to tidy up what he considers the disorder of Russia's democratic experiment. This includes the following: Smashing the oligarchs. He does not want competing centers of power and that means he does not want rich people outside of government who can challenge him, who can support political parties, and opposition candidates. He does not like the idea of a parliament that can actually block what he wants to do. He does not like the idea of a media that can actually investigate what he does, and hold his people to account. He thus wants order without a lot of accountability and without a lot of pluralism.

Boris Nemtsov, one of Yeltsin's former ministers and others confirm that Russia's economic boom has given Putin the cash and support he needs to stamp his authority on the country: "We have $100 billion in the stabilization fund, $300 billion in the central bank, and one great person in the Kremlin who decides how to distribute this unlimited amount of money among the people…do you think such…a system needs democracy? No." Putin is like millions of Russians who have nostalgia for the crazy, bankrupt and corrupted Soviet Union,

---

[5] Washington Post, April 9, 2006

and who don't like freedom and democracy and don't understand the meaning of it."

Further says Nemtsov, Putin has managed to abolish the election of regional governors so that he has tighter control from the center. Parliament is now dominated by a pro-Putin majority that speeds through Kremlin-issued legislation, often too quickly for deputies even to read new bills.

Vladimir Ryzhkov is a legislator who tries to work within the system. He compares the Russian parliament to the toothless Soviet legislature under former leader Leonid Brezhnev. The country is "losing the battle for democracy." "We've been unable to increase press freedom, register opposition parties or have free elections" says Ryzhkov who has introduced legislation to fight corruption, only to have it languish in parliament.

This raises a number of questions: Can we build a modern state without liberty? or based on a government of experts without involvement of the people? Can the government rule without feedback from the society?[6]

---

[6] Think Tank: Transcript for Russian Democracy. Sept 12, 2008.

Democracy Today in Russia

Putin's Plan to Make Russia into a Modern Country

Vladimir Putin became President and principal leader of Russia almost by accident. He was fortunate in developing an association with Boris Yeltsin at a strategically opportune time and in possessing the skills needed by Yeltsin to carry out his goals to scrap Communism and the command economy and to achieve these goals notwithstanding the blunders and burdens placed upon him by a sick and at times bungling Yeltsin.

With the Russian Revolution of 1991 Gorbachev was replaced and Yeltsin assumed power as president of Russia. The USSR was dissolved. Yeltsin had the courage and personality to take control and to abolish Soviet and Communist structures, but lacked the capability of carrying out needed reforms. State property was sold for a fraction of its value to Russian entrepreneurs.[7] Because

---

[7] One such entrepreneur was Boris Abramovich Berezovsky, born January 23, 1946. He was a billionaire and former mathematician. He was a close supporter of Yeltsin and his family. He made a fortune selling Mercedes automobiles and helped Putin enter the Yeltsin inner circle or "family." He then took a strong ownership position with Sibneft and ORT, the country's main TV channel. He went into opposition when Putin became

it brought chaos to the market place, democracy was not working. Corruption and bribery were rife.

In the year 2000 Yeltsin installed his prime minister Vladimir Putin as his successor President. Putin is sober, wiry, acerbic and appears always to be in command; and further, that people are aware that he saved Russia from the ravages of the Yeltsin period. Yeltsin had the image of a bombastic, backslapper who was not inclined to say no to a drink and who let things get out of hand. Some of Yeltsin's admirers say Putin has turned his back on the pluralistic democracy that Yeltsin was seeking to build; but Putin's backers retort that the Yeltsin years sowed instability and a strong hand in the Kremlin was needed to steady the country.[8]

Putin became quite popular and in turn in 2008 installed his own hand picked successor, Dmitry Medvedev who had worked for Putin in St. Petersburg. Medvedev was trained as a lawyer and held a PhD. Putin's popularity stems from changes he brought about in Russia in the last 8 years.[9] When he took office as President in 2000 there were many empty shelves in supermarkets, many political blood feuds and bank collapses. He has given

---

president. He fled the country when accused of defrauding the government of large sums, including $9 million the Russian court in absentia held he had stolen from Aeroflot. Wikipedia.

8 Megan K. Stack, LA Times, Dec. 2, 2007 and Int. Herald Tribune, Sept 16, 2008.

9 Putin's popularity flowed not only from the improvement of the economy but also from Putin's very tough stand against the Chechens who invaded neighbors in the North Caucasus. Russia had severely disabled the Chechen rebel movement.

Russians a sense of stability in contrast to the national shame and chaos left by Yeltsin and his drunken antics. Russia was once again a powerful nation, free from debt, rich in oil and not beholden to the international community.[10]

Thanks to the world wide oil boom[11], pensions have been increased and highly visible swipes have been taken by the government against corruption. Boris Yeltsin was elected President of Russia under a constitution which protected human rights and property and which provided for a separation of powers. In 1992 Yeltsin made a power grab, leading to a military standoff. He was successful in gaining passage of a new constitution which shifted power disproportionately to the executive branch, at the expense of parliament.

In 1996 Yeltsin, though not overly popular, won re-election, thanks to financial help from some of Russia's largest companies which earlier had acquired large and profitable companies from the state. At the same time Yeltsin's health, particularly his heart, was not good, but the press at first had suppressed news of his heart attacks.

While Putin did not ask for this job of running Russia he soon warmed to the challenge and decided that while Russia needed an overhaul, he was the one who under-

---

10 Id.
11 Most of Russia's national income comes from gas and oil and in recent months Russia along with all other oil producing nations has witnessed revenues from these sources plunge, and this may well be followed by more humility from Russia's leaders in dealing with the outside world.

Harold E. Rogers, Jr.

stood Russia's needs at this time and that eight years was not enough time to solve all the many problems which needed to be overcome.

In many ways, the challenges he faced were not unlike those faced by many of his predecessors such as Peter I (the Great), Alexander II, Lenin, Gorbachev or Yeltsin. In each case the then ruler of Russia found himself leading an impoverished nation being left behind on the world stage. Peter I as a young man led a caravan (presumably incognito) to Western Europe and found that by comparison Russia was a backward country where the men all wore long beards and where its defensive and military capabilities left it vulnerable to Western skills and accomplishments. Peter vowed to bring Russia into the next (18th century). He did this by importing military and industrial experts to teach backward Russians how to compete with the West. Russia became drawn into an ill-advised war with England and France in Crimea during the reign of Nicholas I and Alexander II. Russia was defeated and Alexander II and his advisors correctly surmised that Russia had again let itself be outrun and outgunned by Western technology and military maneuvering.[12] Alexander II was also aware that trying to fight with serfs was not helpful in the long run to the Russian cause and he therefore freed the serfs and was about to take other beneficial actions the very day of his death from a terrorists bomb rolled under his carriage not far from his palace.

---

12 See A History of Russia, Bernard Pares, Vintage 1965, p. 357

In the meantime there were great struggles against the totalitarian regime represented by Alexander II, his son Alexander III and grandson Nicholas II, the last Czar. It was Lenin's brother Alexander who was hung for his terrorist activities against the Czar and this of course led to Lenin's vows to get even with his brother's killers. While none of the Russian historical figures mentioned sought to bring democracy to Russia; they all in their way did seek to bring the country out of its particular backward state into one which would provide economic plenty and modernization.

This was true of the actions taken by Gorbachev and Yeltsin. They both wanted to bring about their own perceived version of modernity. Gorbachev knew that Russia was falling well behind other countries of the world and sought to bring about corrections in the command economy and its socialist underpinning. Gorbachev mistakenly thought that he could change the socialism and form of democracy it represented to permit Russia to catch up with the West and to provide a just society producing enough of this world's goods and services to warrant the many changes which would be required in the underlying socialism. Yeltsin on the other hand did not believe the problem could be solved by tinkering with the mechanism providing the goods and services. He rightly understood that the entire mechanism had to be scrapped. He had the guts and the far sightedness to start this process once Gorbachev left office but lacked the skill and good health to carry out all the changes required.

Harold E. Rogers, Jr.

And this is where Putin steps in. He has the vision and health necessary to push the process forward. During the last eight years he has accomplished a great deal but all of his moves have not been moves toward democracy which the West wants him to make. Putin's goal is to transform Russia into a modern country. Certainly that is a worthwhile goal. But the question is: What does it mean to be a modern country? Must it mean that the country is totally democratic? And if it does, what does it mean to be democratic? Stalin used to brag that his Russia was democratic because at elections he could command turnout of voters in the high ninety percent, far more than Western governments could claim.

Also we complain that Putin caused the voting requirements for regional governors to be changed. He reasoned that there was not sufficient control of governors chosen strictly by the local electorate. He proposed a modification of the law permitting the Moscow Center to designate governors, but that they would be then approved by local voters. We would complain that Putin's real goal is to control and squeeze democracy by limiting the freedom of local governors. While that may be the end result there may be other interpretations. In our own democratic history, we have changed the manner in which we select Senators to direct approval by the voters rather than selection by State Legislators. We also have been struggling for many years concerning voting rights of minorities. At the time the original Federal Constitution was adopted blacks (slaves) counted only for 3/5 of value of a white vote and blacks could not vote at all until they were freed and given the franchise by Congress at the end of the Civil War; and it was not until the time of the First World War that women were allowed to vote in America.

And while England has no Supreme Court, Congress or a separate executive branch, we call England a democracy. If there is such a body as a Supreme Court it would be the House of Lords charged with the responsibility of deciding the most serious cases not otherwise disposed of by the House of Commons. And it is the House which debates all important issues and renders a decision. The House likewise becomes the Executive Branch when the majority party is asked by the Queen to form a government with its various ministers called up from its body.

Thus there are many forms of democracy and the definitions are not always the same. Countries throughout the world may claim to be democracies, but may or may not be according to our or their peculiar definitions. Quite often we mean, in determining whether a country qualifies as a democracy some or more of the following: Are all citizens, men and women alike encouraged to vote at general and special elections? At the polling or voting places, are votes only permitted by qualified voters? Is there a fair mechanism to count the votes cast? Does the State or local government take all reasonable measures to make sure necessary voting materials are available in sufficient quantities and form to yield a fair election.? Is the court system fair and proper, so that citizens can rest assured that procedural and other laws are adopted by proper votes rather than decree? Can citizens believe that judges will be fairly compensated and that they cannot be influenced to cast a vote based on a bribe?

In a strong liberal tradition can citizens believe that their personal rights will be observed such as not being arrested without proper warrants based on evidence and can they be entitled to a fair trial at which they have adequate and competent representation and that they can only be convicted based on proper evidence; that they will be given a fair and speedy trial; and that their property will not be taken without due process?.
A democratic society is one in which there is freedom to speak and write; one in which means of communication are equally available to government and citizens to permit them to get their message out without penalty. This would include freedom of the press, and of all television media.

Most leaders and rulers including Putin would like to have the unfettered freedom to rule without being called to account by the electorate. However if corruption is to be avoided, the corrupt must be subject to the bright light of inquiry such as we see on our television sets and in our newspapers on a daily basis. Putin of course does not like the idea of rich people outside government, having the financial means to challenge his actions or statements. There is something to be said for having a strong executive run an army in the midst of a battle. There must be a general in charge of the colonels and lower officers and troops to carry out the decisions made by those in charge. Certainly it is far more efficient to have orders issued and obeyed without question, or perhaps without too many questions being asked. But the first question to be settled is Who is the Boss?, Whose rights are being furthered? Thus if there is any serious question about what should be done or how it should be done, Who should prevail?, Is the (Russian) Citizen's interest being furthered or is it that of the Ruler?

Putin's Background and Qualifications for Presidency

To the extent that Putin is now serving or will continue to serve the interests of the Russian people in a democratic manner, his background and qualifications become relevant. The people should scrutinize these qualifications as in any democracy to determine if Putin should continue to be hired to carry out the people's business. Likewise Putin's predecessors provide a critical history showing the cultural, political and economic context which either overtly or silently controls the manner in which Putin and his predecessors made choices as to what issues they considered critical and how they historically or in the future would decide their own or what they perceive to be Russia's best interests.

Vladimir Vladimirovich Putin was born in 1952 and was a political protégé of Boris Yeltsin. Putin's father served in the Soviet navy and was assigned to the submarine fleet. His paternal grandfather had been the personal cook for both Lenin and Stalin. His father was a militant atheist but his mother was an orthodox Christian who attended church regularly and who had her son Vladimir secretly christened when he was a baby. He is regularly shown on television attending Orthodox services.[13] He graduated in 1975 from the law school at the university of St. Petersburg and thereafter obtained a doctorate in economics. Putin is fluent in German. He has taken English lessons and has talked directly to President Bush at some of their meetings. However for formal talks he will speak through and interpreter.

Following school he was recruited by the KGB and joined the communist party. In the KGB he was assigned to combat political dissent and to ferret out foreign intelligence. He worked for the KGB for 15 years (earning the rank of lieutenant colonel) and completed a tour of duty in Dresden, East Germany. One of his law school professors was Anatoli Sobchak who later became Mayor of St. Petersburg. Upon his return from Dresden, Putin was hired by Sobchak to head up the St. Petersburg's office of foreign affairs. His responsibilities included advising Sobchak on international affairs and promoting international relations and foreign investments. One of Putin's assistants was Dmitry Medvedev, now his successor as President of Russia. In 1996 Yeltsin transferred Putin to Moscow. He had developed a reputation as intelligent, tough and hard working. In 1998 Yeltsin appointed him head of the Federal Security Service (FSB), successor to the KGB. In 1999 he took over the duties of Sergei Stepashin as Prime Minister. He became popular with many Russians for his September 1999 invasion of Chechnya in response to terrorism there. He became acting president when Yeltsin resigned that post.

---

13 Wikipedia contains general support for most of the factual assertions in this paper.

Putin's Prompt Actions after Appointment as President

Putin moved quickly to reestablish the authority of the central government over the Russian republics and administrative units. He also increased control over the independent media. In addition he sought to revamp and reduce the size of the Russian military. He pushed economic reforms through parliament and renewed ties with former Soviet client states. He reinstated opposition to US ballistic missile defenses. His economic and legal reforms helped stabilize the government and the economy. His first Decree, signed on December 31, 1999 was one which guaranteed that corruption charges against Yeltsin and his family would not be pursued. He was re-elected president in March, 2004.[14]

Changes in the law which he promoted after the Beslan school terrorist attack allowed him to appoint regional and provincial governors, increasing power of the central government over the federation's constituents. His second term as president was marked by increasing government control over Russian oil and gas, and economic retaliation against nations which clashed politically with Russia. Under Putin there also has been a gradual contraction of freedom of the press. Russia has taken a much more aggressive stance against the US, noticeable particularly at an anti American tirade in Munich.[15]

---

14 The Columbia Encyclopedia, 2001-08
15 The speech was given by Putin in February 2007 at the annual Munich Conference on Security Policy. He criticized what he called the United States' monopolistic dominance in global rela-

Harold E. Rogers, Jr.

Putin's Personal Finances

According to disclosures made by Putin during the legislative elections, his personal wealth consists of about $150,000 in bank accounts, a private apartment in St. Petersburg, some bank stock and several antique automobiles. His official annual income is about $80,000. However, The British Guardian newspaper[16] contends that Putin controls a personal fortune worth at least $40 billion hidden in Switzerland and Liechtenstein. The source of this claim is Stanislav Belkovsky, a Russian political expert. The claim has also been made through other newspapers including Die Welt, the Washington Post and Moscow Times. Putin's claimed assets (effective control) include 37% of the shares of Surgutneftegaz, (about $20 billion) Russia's third largest oil producer, 4.5% of Gazprom (about $13 billion) and at least 50% of Gunvor, a Swiss based oil trader formed by Putin's friend Gennady Timchenko. Putin's name does not appear on any shareholder register.

The Kremlin and Putin have refused to comment on the Guardian's claims. Although such questions have been

---

tions, and stated that the US showed an "almost uncontained hyper use of force in international relations" He added that "no one feels safe! Because no one can feel that international law is like a stone wall that will protect them. Of course such a policy stimulates an arms race." He called for a "fair and democratic world order that would ensure security and prosperity not only for a select few, but for all": In a January, 2007 interview Putin said Russia is in favor of a democratic multipolar world and of strengthening the system of international law. Wikipedia.

16 www.guardian.co.uk/world/12/21/2007

taboo, information began to leak out of a fight over control of Kremlin assets as preparations were made to transfer powers of the Presidency to Dmitry Medvedev. The fight was between a hard line group led by Igor Sechin, Putin's deputy chief of staff and a liberal clan which includes Medvedev. The Sechin group is made up of silovki, (Kremlin officials with security and military backgrounds) This group includes Nikolai Patruchev, head of the FSB, successor to the KGB and Alexander Bortnikov his deputy and Putin's aide Viktor Ivanov. Members of the liberal group include Roman Abramovich who is close to the Yeltsin family, and Viktor Cherkesov head of the federal drug control service and Alisher Usmanov. Kremlin insiders say the battle is like a war between business competitors, not one relating to ideology.

When Putin was asked about some of these claims at a press conference on February 14, 2008, he dodged answering directly but said that it is true that he is rich, but that is because citizens have bestowed great trust in him. But concerning rumors of financial wealth: "I have seen some pieces of paper regarding this. This is plain chatter, not worthy."

Putin's Agenda

An analysis of Putin's speeches and press conferences helps us see and organize the Agenda he and Medvedev are likely to pursue. Fighting corruption is at the top of both Putin's and Medvedev's list and is likely to be the most difficult to achieve since corruption is so ingrained in the makeup of Russian society. However Russia is not the only nation struggling with corruption. Recent news comes from our State of Illinois that steps are being taken to impeach the Governor for offering for sale a US Senate seat vacated by President Barak Obama. Demands for his resignation seem to fall on his deaf ears and the Governor does not think there is anything wrong in his receiving a quid pro quo for designating the next US Senator of Illinois. Putin and Medvedev have referred to all of the Agenda items listed below, but clearly although their intentions might be good, they will run out of time before they achieve all their various goals or will find these goals worthy but unachievable or good for public statements but not for concrete achievements.

Each of these agenda items may be discussed or referred to in the text of this paper, but some items, like corruption, consume more discussion time than others. The achievement of some of the goals may occur through actions (meetings with foreign heads of state (Cuba and Venezuela for example) or through statements in speeches (the Putin speech at Munich demanding more respect for Russia[17] and the multipolar world), or announcements of Russian placement of missiles in Kaliningrad.

Fight Corruption

Strengthen rule of law[18]

---

17 On August 18, 2008 Medvedev declared to veterans in Kursk that we (Russia) "simply want respect, respect for our country, our people and our values." He also claimed that Russia had never been the first to attack any country.

18 The rule of law is a fundamental component of a democratic society and is defined broadly as the principle that all members of society—both citizens and rulers—are bound by a set of

Further Sovereign Democracy[19]

Adopt Democratic Procedures

Carry Out Kyoto Protocol by cleaning environment[20]

---

clearly defined and universally accepted laws. In a democracy, the rule of law is manifested in an independent judiciary, a free press and a system of checks and balances on leaders through free elections and separation of powers among the branches of government. Further the government is bound by the law; all people are treated equally under the law; and the law recognizes that in each person, there is a core of spirituality and dignity and humanity.(US Dept of State).

19 According to public opinion polls conducted by the Levada Center, Putin's approval rating is 81%, the highest of any world leader, up from 31% in August 1999. Observers see his high approval ratings as a consequence of higher living standards and Russia's reassertion of itself on the world scene.

But there are also detractors to Putin. However critics are seldom seen on major national TV which is now controlled by the Kremlin. Putin in rebuttal has stated that some domestic critics are being funded by foreign enemies who would prefer to see a weak Russia. In a speech at United Russia in Luzhniki he stated: "Those who would oppose us don't want us to realize our plan…They need a weak, sick state! They need a disorganized and disoriented society, a divided society, so that they can do their deeds behind its back and eat cake on our table" Wikipedia

20 In 2004 Putin signed the Kyoto Protocol treaty designed to reduce green house gasses.

Harold E. Rogers, Jr.

Negotiate for Multipolar[21] world[22]

Complete negotiations for military security of borders[23]

Fight national epidemics of AIDS and alcoholism

Control Oligarchs and recover State Property

Strengthen internal power[24]

21 Prior to the G-8 summit on June 4, 2007 Putin said: "we do not want confrontation; we want to engage in dialogue. However, we want a dialogue that acknowledges the equality of both parties' interests."

22 In September 2007 Putin visited Indonesia, the first Russian leader to do so in 50 years. He also visited Tehran, Iran and met with President Ahmadinejad and with other leaders of the Caspian Sea area. On October 26, 2007 Putin visited Portugal and proposed creating a Russian European Institute for Freedom and Democracy headquartered in Europe and announced: "we are ready to supply funds for financing" This institute would monitor human rights violation in Europe.

23 Putin announced on August 17, 2007 the resumption on a permanent basis of long distance patrol flights of Russia's strategic bombers that were suspended in 1992. This followed the 2007 Peace Mission where Chinese and Russian military exercises were conducted jointly by SCO member states. And by an announcement of the Russian Defense Minister on December 5, 2007 that 11 ships, including the aircraft carrier Kuznetzov would take part in a major navy sortie into the Mediterranean since Soviet times. The sortie would be backed up by 47 aircraft, including strategic bombers.

24 Putin is taking various steps including re-writing highschool history books to show Russian history, particularly Stalin in a

Strengthen State Capitalism[25] and financial power[26]

Rebuild State infrastructure for transport, schools and public buildings

Increase social benefits for medical services, pension and related benefits

---

more favorable light. These new school manuals state that Stalin was "the most successful Soviet leader ever."
Putin himself is being elevated in the minds of Russian citizens, suggesting a new trend toward cult of personality. In December, 2007 Putin commandeered a sports stadium and threw a combination political rally and rock concert with the sole purpose of praising, as the massive banners proclaimed "the glory of Putin" Putin himself appeared as the keynote speaker. LA Times, Dec. 2, 2007. This type of political rally is somewhat new to the West, but not dissimilar to a gigantic rally held by President Elect Obama in Denver during the recent election campaign.

25 The Yukos affair below is seen by the Western Press as a sign of a broader shift toward a system normally described as state capitalism where the entirety of state-owned and controlled enterprises are run by and for the benefit of the group around the leader (Putin); a collection of former KGB colleagues, St. Petersburg lawyers and other associates and friends.

26 The flow of petrodollars was the foundation of Putin's regime. Oil and gas account for 50% of Russian budget revenues and 65% of its exports. Russia is thus quite vulnerable to the rapid fluctuations of the oil and gas market. But Russia has created stabilization and other reserve funds to protect it from anticipated shocks.

Organized Crime and Corruption and Other Matters for the Russian Agenda

Corruption and bribe taking has become a way of life in Russia. Bribes are routinely requested of business men and just as routinely paid as a cost of doing business. Bribery is the most prevalent crime in Russia. In 1993 almost half of those charged with bribery were government officials and more than half that number were law enforcement officers. Such officers also entered into illicit partnerships with organized crime and clandestine business groups. Mafia members are engaged in crime both in Russia and America and are engaged in theft, extortion, money laundering, gun trafficking, drug running, prostitution, smuggling, load sharking, contract killing and other crimes.

The US Department of Justice has established special task forces to deal with the Russian Mafia in New York, Los Angeles and Miami. US businesses which pay bribes and protection money in Russia may unwittingly be financing Russian criminal activity in the US. Bribery of Russian government officials undercuts efforts to create an open and democratic government in Russia. A cornerstone of US foreign policy is to help democracy take root and flourish in Russia and thus the US should not tolerate support of corrupt officials as Russia changes from a corrupt totalitarian regime to a popular democracy.

US citizens are governed by the Foreign Corrupt Practices Act which prohibits payment of bribes and other illicit payments to government officials. However this Act has not been vigorously enforced because, among other reasons, cooperation of the offending government is required for a successful prosecution. Also payments made to insure timely compliance (grease payments) are exempt. While all industrialized nations prohibit bribery of their own officials, only the US prohibits bribery of foreign government officials. Payments to a third party for the purpose of paying a bribe to a foreign official are also prohibited if the payer has knowledge of the illicit nature of the payment.

The Russian market is virtually unregulated and has created a wealth of opportunities for criminal organizations ranging from the shake down of small kiosk operators for protection money, to the peddling of stolen nuclear fuel on the international market. Official corruption is rampant.[27] 1994 polls showed that only fourteen percent of Russians living in Moscow believed Russia to be a democracy and nearly a forth of those polled believed that organized crime, not the Government runs the country.

---

27 Fordham International Law Journal (Vol. 19, 1999, 1996) Scott P. Boylan

DEMOCRACY TODAY IN RUSSIA

Russian criminal organizations threaten government authority. Bank managers have requested government protection. Those who fail to cooperate with organized crime have been routinely assassinated. Thus Russians have equated democracy with lawlessness and a sharp decrease in personal safety.

The Russian Duma has struggled to come up with a crime bill which gives the government effective power to track down and punish criminals, but which will not deprive citizens of basic rights of self defense. During the pre Communist revolution years (1917) the Czarist governments adopted stringent crime laws which greatly restricted civil rights.[28] Crime and its impact on the development of democracy has been a primary concern of many Russian politicians. Many members fear that Russia will become a criminalized society if adequate economic reform is not adopted and corrupt influences are not eliminated. Putin has been very much aware of these fears and thus has made elimination of chaos and corruption as one of his central goals[29].

Members of organized crime groups have sought to infiltrate Duma to take advantage of immunity from criminal prosecution. During Russia's Soviet period the Communist Party was largely seen as the most powerful of all criminal organizations, controlling not just one aspect of an illicit economy but rather the whole nation and its resources. In 1994 the Russian government reported that seventy to eighty percent of private business-

---
28 See generally Comrade Criminal, Stephen Handelman, Yale University Press, 1995
29 Jamestown Foundation, Pavel K. Baev (5-22-06)

es were paying extortion money to organized criminal gangs.. The growth of organized crime has severely hampered the growth of private small businesses in Russia. In 1993 organized crime controlled forty percent of the turnover in goods and services in Russia, according to the Russian Ministry of Internal Affairs. US companies and individuals doing business in Russia became a target of Russian criminals.

It is estimated that twenty percent of all foreigners engaged in business in St. Petersburg have paid protection money to the Russian Mafia. They either pay, (risking getting caught for US violations) expend large sums for security or leave Russia.

After years of corruption and crony capitalism,[30] Putin is attempting through ongoing investigations to discover crimes of corruption, to regain control of the Russian economy and impose the rule of law. Such investigations will also allow the government to recover assets that were stolen, especially during the Yeltsin period and at the same time attempt to reassure foreign investors that corruption will not be tolerated. Putin now will need to build a firewall between his allies and foes. He must now decide whether to let his allies fall in the name of the law, or protect them and undermine his campaign and his own authority.[31]

---

[30] Russia has a long history of bribe taking and according to Indem Foundation which monitors corruption in Russia, Russians spend 10 times more in bribes today than they did four years ago, the average bribe paid by business people to keep their businesses running smoothly has risen 13 times in four years from a total of $33.5 billion in 2001 to $316 billion

[31] www.LA_times.com, p 7/13/2000

DEMOCRACY TODAY IN RUSSIA

At the time Putin negotiated the handover of the Presidency to Medvedev, the exact sharing of duties had not been worked out. However each of Putin and Medvedev conducted press conferences[32] and speeches from time to time and it appeared that Medvedev will take the lead in law matters and certain domestic goals. In one of his campaign speeches[33] Medvedev advocated private property, economic deregulation, low taxes, an independent judiciary, anti-corruption and defending personal freedoms. One of his campaign themes was use of the phrase "Freedom is better than non-freedom."[34]

---

32 Putin had become quite skilled at fielding questions for more than 3 hours phoned in to Moscow. Reuters, Dec. 4, 2008. Medvedev does not yet have the same confidence with such conferences as Putin.

33 Medvedev has promised to improve schools, build housing, encourage business and amend the tax code to encourage household and social stability, including offering tax breaks for retirement savings, charitable donations and education and medical costs. His agenda overlaps Putin's, particularly in promises to fight corruption and reversing the poor state of public health. NY Times, Feb 28, 2008.

34 In a speech on Feb 15, 2008 Medvedev said that liberty was necessary for the state to have legitimacy among its citizens. He has articulated domestic policy goals as if he were communicating to Russia's expanding consumer class. Sergei Markov, a member of Parliament and close to the Kremlin expects that Medvedev will push for more political freedom and will encourage political competition without destabilizing the system. Medvedev's political competitors for the presidency were Gennadi A. Zyuganov, the Communist candidate, Andrei V. Bogdanov, the almost unknown candidate of the Democratic Party and Vladimir V. Zhirinovsky, an ultranationalist. They are remnants of an organized opposition which, it has been suggested are run by the Kremlin to create the appearance of a race.

Harold E. Rogers, Jr.

On August 31, 2008 Medvedev announced a shift in Russian foreign policy built on five main principles:

Fundamental principles of international law are supreme.
The world will be multipolar
Russia will not seek confrontation with other nations.
Russia will protect its citizens wherever they are
Russia will develop ties in friendly regions.

Medvedev appears to be more liberal than Putin. Both attended law school at the University of St. Petersburg. Medvedev (Dmitry Anatolyevich) was born on September 14, 1965. Medvedev was inaugurated President of Russia on May 7, 2008, following winning the Presidential election on March 2, 2008 with about 70% of the vote. He had never held elective office before, but won by virtue of recommendation for the post by Putin and by a carefully orchestrated campaign mainly conducted on national television. He grew up in St. Petersburg in a 430 square foot flat, the son of two university professors. He is fond of sports and a fan of English bands Black Sabbath and Deep Purple.

Medvedev's wife Svetlana, was his school sweetheart. They have a son born in 1996. Medvedev studied at and received a PhD in law from the University of St. Petersburg. He worked under Putin in St. Petersburg from 1991 to 1996 working as an expert for the International Relations Committee. In 1999 Putin brought Medvedev to Moscow and in December, 1999 he was appointed deputy head of the presidential staff. During the 2000 elections he was Putin's campaign manager. From 2000 to 2001 he was chairman of Gazprom's board of directors. In October, 2003 he became presidential chief of staff. In December, 2007 Putin announced that Medvedev was his preferred successor and thereafter he was confirmed as their candidate by the political party, United Russia. Following his party endorsement Medvedev announced that Putin would be his prime minister to head the Russian government.

Medvedev has written articles for Russian law journals and co-authored a textbook on civil law published in 1991. He also authored a textbook concerning the role of the Russian state in social policy and economic development and is co-author of a book of legal commentary, to be published in 2008. This book considers Russian Federal law and Civil service.

In his first address to the Russian parliament on November 5, 2008 he proposed a change in the Russian Constitution increasing the terms of the President and State Duma from four to six and five years respectively. This change would legalize Putin's desire to serve a longer term. He also promised to deploy the Iskander missile system and radar-jamming facilities in Kaliningrad to counter the US missile defense system in Eastern Europe. This deployment will send a strong message to the West that Russia has the will and the clout to crowd the East European borders with missiles, just as the West seeks to locate missiles in Poland and Czechoslovakia.[35]

---

35 Putin did attempt to negotiate with President Bush, offering

Criticism Of Nemtsov, Milov And Others

Clearly Putin deserves many of the accolades he has received for his accomplishments during the first eight years as leader and president. Compared to the chaos of the Yeltsin period and the economic plenty which many Russians are experiencing, his detractors do not have the strong case against his rule that they had once thought. One of the sharpest attacks on the Putin record came in the form of a brief book entitled <u>Putin: the Results</u> written by Bois Nemtsov and Vladimir Milov. A review of the report was made by Amy Knight and published May 15, 2008. Putin made a speech to the State Council on February 8, 2008 in which he took credit for the stability his government had established. "People once more have confidence that life will continue to change for the better." A few days later at a press conference Putin said: "I have worked like a galley slave throughout these eight years, morning till night, and I have given all I could to this work. I am happy with the results." He was also buoyed by the 70% vote victory achieved by Medvedev in the Presidential race.

---

to share and upgrade radar facilities located in Azerbaijan, but Bush turned him down. Wikipedia

DEMOCRACY TODAY IN RUSSIA

Nemtsov and Milov are highly regarded liberal democrats with inside knowledge of the Kremlin. Nemtsov has a Ph.D. in physics and mathematics and was a popular governor of Nizhny-Novgorod. He then served as first deputy prime minister of Russia under Yeltsin. He was co-founder of the Union of Right Forces and was a member of the Duma. Milov is a respected energy specialist and worked as deputy minister of energy in 2002. He designed market reforms for the Russian gas, electricity and railway industries. He is now head of an Energy think tank. Their book presents a devastating picture of Putin's 8 years as president and the Kremlin attempted to block its distribution.

In his February 8, 2008 speech, Putin asserted that his administration had enormous success bringing the people new prosperity and in tackling problems inherited from the chaotic Yeltsin presidency. When he took office Chechnya was a "regime of terror" planning to carry out aggression against Russia. Russian armed forces, demoralized and under equipped, were not prepared for combat. The government was weak and ineffective, with little regard for the law. Agriculture was in a state of crisis. The economy was controlled by oligarchs and criminal organizations. Inflation was running at 36.5 percent and unprecedented amounts of wages, pensions, and benefits were not being paid.

Today, in contrast, according to Putin, the war in the North Caucasus is over and Chechnya has a full fledged democracy. Russia's levels of social and economic development have been rising. Citizens can exercise their rights in full and courts enjoy real independence. Total investment in the Russian economy has increased sevenfold. Real incomes are 2.5 times what they were in 2000. Also Russia has a stable and effective political system. Nemtsov and Milov acknowledge the economic successes including the 70% rise in Russia's GDP since Putin came to power. Much of this increase is however due to the relatively high price of oil and gas. The excess revenue should have been used by the Kremlin, according to the authors, to carry out much needed reforms in health care, education, transportation, the pension system and army. However as under Brezhnev, this excess income has been largely frittered away. The authors also point out that there is unprecedented corruption draining off available surpluses. Regarding corruption, in 2007 Russia as a country ranked a low of 143rd worldwide.[36]

Nemtsov and Milov assert that assets are being removed from state ownership and handed over to the control of private individuals. Also property is being repurchased with state money from the oligarchs at stunning prices. A "friends of Putin" oil export monopoly is being created and a Kremlin "black safe" (slush fund) is being funded. The authors claim that government assets including the insurance subsidiary of Gazprom, Sogz, its pension funds and its mass media interests have fallen into the hands of Rossiya Bank. For example the Media Holdings subsidiary was acquired in 2005 for only $166 million and within two years Medvedev, chairman of Gazprom, valued these holdings at $7.5 billion,

---

[36] See Transparency International.

a price increase of some 45 times the earlier acquisition price. Another asset (75% of the shares of Sibneft) was acquired from Roman Abramovich, now living in the UK for $13.7 billion. Abramovich bought the shares in 1995 for only $100 million. The authors acknowledge that Kremlin financial records are kept secret and thus it is difficult to verify asset purchase and sales prices.

The authors argue that the excess profits earned from these assets should have been used to pay for more needful projects, such as repairing the road system, and public health needs. Regarding public health, the life expectancy for Russian men is less than 59 years in large part because of the rise of smoking and alcohol abuse (Russia has an estimated 2.5 million alcoholics) Traffic fatalities have also increased 60% since 2000. In addition violent crime rose by 170% between 2000 and 2006. The Russian health care system is in crisis. Because of insufficient funds, poorly equipped hospitals, shortages of medicines and widespread bribe taking for medical services, health care in any reasonable quality is beyond the reach of most Russians. In the meantime the quality of Russia's education is declining, affordable housing is scarce and the pension system is headed for a collapse. In 2005 Putin introduced the National Projects to be supervised by Medvedev. This program would allocate money for improving health care, education, housing and agriculture. But little has been heard of this initiative since it was launched..

According to the authors, a grave failure of Putin's leadership has been the decline in the rule of law and respect for human rights. With the exception of the lower courts, the country's judges are entirely subordinate to those in political power. Instead of protecting civil rights, law enforcement agencies and courts use the law to advance the financial interests of powerful political clans. As in the case with Mikhail Khodorkovsky, former owner of Yukos, tax terrorism is used by the government to take over ownership of property from private owners and redistribute it to Kremlin insiders.

Because of controls the government has on the media, it will be difficult for opponents to get their message out to bring about changes in the law. Many of the corrections Nemtsov and Milov have urged call for a reallocation of the national budget to make changes as any democratic parliament would make. First comes a charge from the opposition party that expenditures should be made according to their plan. A full and fair debate then follows and finally a vote. Where Russia in this case is deficient is with the media and the right of citizens to express their views and enforce their will against the party in power. The Kremlin virtually controls all mass media, particularly National television which is the most potent media force in Russia, and perhaps even the US and Western Europe. As for the print media, there are only three truly independent daily newspapers in Russia, Novaya Gazeta, Kommersant and Vedomosti and together they have a very small circulation. With respect to radio, Ekho Moskvy is provocative, but others stick to the Kremlin line. The internet is not yet censored, but less than 20% of adult Russians regularly go on line. Because of the difficulties for communication by Russian liaberals, they have reverted to protests and street demonstrations.

Nemtsov believes that change will have to come from Russians themselves and that Putin made an invisible contract with the Russian people by which they tolerate corruption, mismanagement, crime, and constraints on the mass media so long as they have buying power and continue to live better than they did in the Yeltsin era. However if the economy falters, that invisible contract could be broken.[37]

---

37 If there is a crisis, the electorate may demand accountability. There presently are signs of economic vulnerability, with the cost of living rising sharply and inflation reaching 12.6% in January 2008.

Russian History and Culture which will guide Putin

When Vladimir Putin took the helm of the Russian ship of state, it was about to careen off course and crash on dangerous rocks jutting out into the sea. Putin's immediate tasks were to steer a course which would save the ship and take steps he thought would keep the ship on a proper course given changing local and world events. He was criticized for taking some steps deemed less than democratic but also cheered by many Russians who found their lives steadily improving after the chaos of the Yeltsin years.

For the future Putin as prime minister, and Medvedev as president must continue to keep the Russian ship of state on course, but in addition are charged with the responsibility of carrying out the program set forth in the party charter and the promises made to the voters when they were voted into office. How they go about this task and what tasks they undertake will depend not only on the state of the world and of Russia from time to time, but more likely on the history and the historical culture handed to them by their predecessors. Putin, for example, did not invent Communism, but he had to deal with and control it if Russian society were to be improved. It is important for us, therefore, to know something about the Russian leaders and Russian history which Putin inherited and why, in order for us to be able to understand events and problems today.

In order to better understand the challenges and opportunities presented to Putin and his successors, I will outline such challenges and discuss them, beginning with Stalin. It was Stalin and his statement of Communism which left such an imprint on Russian society, part of which culture continues even today but much of which has been or is being torn apart (perestroika) to make way for the new Russian society. Likewise we will look to history beginning with Stalin (perhaps the inspiration for the term "evil empire") because he did not purport to give Russian society democracy or anything like democracy, whereas his successors (at least most of them) sought to give the appearance that they were going to improve life for Russian citizens. The first Russian ruler after Stalin was Krushchev who took some important steps to open society by exposing many of Stalin's most hateful activities, but clearly did not take steps toward democracy.

Joseph Stalin

Joseph Stalin was born in the City of Gori, Soviet Georgia on December 21 1879. He died on March 5, 1953. He was the son of a shoemaker and initially pursued a career in the priesthood, but failed in this endeavor when he was expelled from the seminary he attended for inability to pay school fees and for missing final exams. His birth name was Iosif Vissasrionovich Dzhugashvili but as a young revolutionary he adopted the name Stalin which means Man of Steel. Stalin's father became an alcoholic which led among other things to the failure of his business. He became violently abusive to his wife and young son. The town where Stalin grew up was also violent and lawless. At age 10 he enrolled in the Gori Church School where most of his peers were sons of affluent priests, officials and merchants. Stalin was a good student, earning top marks and had a good singing voice. His father was furious when he was accepted at the Gori school, because he wanted him to become a cobbler. He graduated first in his class at age 16, despite his father's refusal to support his mother and pay school fees. He received a scholarship to the Seminary in Tiflis and gained some fame as a poet.

But he also was drawn into studying forbidden literature, including Marxism for which he was caught and punished. He was harassed and spied upon and became and atheist. In 1898 he joined the Russian Social Democratic Labor Party from which the Bolsheviks were later formed. Soon after leaving school Stalin discovered the writings of Lenin and decided to become a revolutionary. In the early days of the Communist revolution he met and joined with Lenin and thus became his Bolshevik co-conspirator. Stalin and Lenin both attended the Fifth Congress of the Russian Social Democratic Labour Party in London in 1907. This Congress debated strategy for communist revolution in Russia. Stalin began organizing major criminal activities including bank robberies to finance party activities. For a time he was editor of Pravda. He was also arrested at various times and shipped off to Siberia from which he managed to escape. He rose to power in 1922 as Secretary General of the Communist Party. Using his administrative skills and ruthless maneuvering, Stalin rid himself of potential rivals, first by having many condemned as deviationists and later ordering them executed.[38]

One of his principal rivals was Leon Trotsky whom he had expelled from the party and then pursued to Mexico where he was murdered. To solidify his position and to advance his goal of socialism in one country, he put the Soviet Union on a crash course of collectivization and industrialization. Some 25 million farmers were forced onto state farms and some 14.5 million people were killed as a result of collectivization, while agricultural output was reduced by 25 per cent according to some estimates. The Russian Civil War and wartime communism contributed to the devastating effect Stalin's reforms had on the country's economy. Industrial output in 1922 was 13% of that in 1914. Stalin replaced the New Economic Policy with Five Year Plans beginning in 1928. These provided for state guided crash industrialization and collectivization of agriculture.

In the 1930's Stalin launched his Great Purge[39], ridding the party of all the people who had brought him to power. It has been estimated that more than half the party or in excess of 1.2 million members were arrested between 1936 and 1939. Of these 600,000 died by tor-

---

[38] For general background see Stalin and the Shaping of the Soviet Union, Alex DeJonge, William Morrow, NY 1986; See also CNN Interactive for Joseph Stalin. See also Wikipedia.

[39] See Wikipedia for general background on Purges.

ture, execution, or died in the Gulag[40] Stalin made a serious strategic error when he purged the officer corps of the Soviet Armed Forces and was unprepared for the war when Hitler double crossed him by attacking the USSR on June 22, 1941. Stalin had signed a secret non-aggression pact with Nazi Germany in August, 1939. For two weeks after the attack Stalin was not seen nor heard from. However Stalin took charge of the troops at the end of this period.

Since Hitler had now taken on nearly the whole world, Stalin joined with the Allies also fighting Hitler, meeting to work out a coordinated strategy with British Prime Minister Winston Churchill and US President Franklin D. Roosevelt at Tehran in 1943, Yalta in 1945 and with President Harry S. Truman in Potsdam at the end of the war, following Roosevelt's death. At these meetings, the allied parties reached agreements to divide the postwar world into spheres of influence. Roosevelt had died suddenly in April, 1945 of a heart attack, but he was clearly not well during the Yalta meeting and there is general consensus that he was out maneuvered by Stalin and that he needlessly gave up effective control of Eastern Europe.

---

40 Early research attempting to count the number of people killed under Stalin's regime placed the number of victims in a range of 3 to 60 million. But following dissolution of the Soviet Union in 1991, the archives show that about 800,000 prisoners were executed under Stalin for either political or criminal offenses, while about 1.7 million died in the Gulag and some 390,000 perished during kulak forced resettlement, or a total of about 3 million victims.

The allied forces, principally the US, anticipated that based on Japanese willingness to die as a kamikaze pilot or otherwise, to save the Japanese home land and that the US might suffer at least a million casualties in the attempt to conquer the homeland. Roosevelt made a deal with Stalin that the USSR would join the fight against Japan in exchange for accepting Soviet control of Eastern Europe (but on the assumption that new governments would be chosen in democratic elections). Stalin did join the fight against Japan in August, 1945, but did not carry out free democratic elections and Roosevelt was not around to make sure he did. Also in August, 1945 Truman authorized dropping the first nuclear bomb on Japan at Hiroshima and Nagasaki and Japan surrendered. Stalin wanted to expand his influence in the Far East, particularly the Kurile Islands, Southern Sakhalin and Northern Korea.. Stalin sought to build buffer zones around his territorial boundaries, particularly to establish like minded regimes around his borders. Winston Churchill described these border arrangements as an iron curtain.

To help the nations of Europe get back on their feet, following destruction of their cities, industries and other facilities, the US offered the Marshall Plan in 1947. At first Stalin approved participation of East European nations, but then forbade it. The USSR was denied access to West Germany and therefore Stalin agreed to the formation of the German Democratic Republic (GDR) in 1949. The increasingly hostile relations between the West and the USSR brought about a status described as the Cold War. In the arrangements negotiated at the end of the War, the British, US, France and USSR were all given specific territories to occupy, including specific areas of the City of Berlin. In the early 1950's Stalin tried to freeze out the Western occupying forces by prohibiting rail and highway access. The West countered by flying supplies to Berlin and eventually broke the blockade. In another ploy, but by Stalin's successors, the Soviets tried to stop the escape of citizens to the West and therefore caused a high wall to be built around the USSR occupied zone to prevent escape. However escapes continued and eventually the Soviets (now led by Gorbachev) realized that they could not win and the wall was ordered torn down.

Nikita Sergeyevich Khrushchev

Nikita S. Khrushchev was born in 1894 to an illiterate peasant family in a village near the Russian-Ukraine border. Although he held two jobs, his father could not earn enough income to feed his family so he moved his family to an industrial center in Ukraine in 1908. Nikita began working in a factory and by age 18 had joined other workers organizing a strike to protest working conditions. Although fired from his first job, Khrushchev remained active as a strike organizer. In 1917 following ousting of the Czar, he joined the Bolsheviks and served as a political commissar. Following the Bolshevik victories Khrushchev was sent to a Technical College to study Marxism. Upon graduation he was appointed to a political post in Ukraine where he met friends of Stalin. He joined Lazar Kaganovich and supported his struggles with Stalin against Leon Trotsky. With Stalin's victory, Khrushchev's career soared. By 1935 he was second in command of the Moscow Communist party. He was given general oversight of construction of the Moscow subway system and by 1939 he became a full member of the Politburo.

During the 1930's Stalin began a series of bloody purges to consolidate his power. Krushchev was drawn into the purges as an accomplice and denounced several fellow students and workers as enemies of the people. He willingly took part in the extermination of the Ukrainian intelligentsia. Nazi Germany invaded Russia in 1941 and Krushchev was sent to head the Communist party in Ukraine where he witnessed the devastation of the war first hand. By the time of Stalin's death in 1953 Krushchev was one of Stalin's top advisors. He and Nikolai Bulganin won a power struggle against Georgi Malenkov and Lavrenti Beria, resulting in the resignation of Malenkov and execution of Beria.

Krushchev became the dominant figure as head of the Communist Party and at the 20th Party Congress in 1956 Krushchev made a broad scale attack on Stalin and his crimes, carefully avoiding any mention of his own complicity. Satellite countries of Eastern Europe began to assert their independence from Communist Russia and the Soviet system. While Krushchev promoted change, he could not tolerate dissent. He sent Soviet tanks and troops to Budapest to brutally suppress the Hungarian rebellion. His tenure was marked by several high stakes crises including the U-2 Spy plane affair which resulted in the cancellation of a summit between the US and the USSR, the building of the Berlin Wall and the Cuban Missile crises.

Krushchev embarrassed his Party and government with some frequency with his pugnacious and intemperate behavior. For example he bragged to Vice President Nixon during a now famous Moscow fair, that the Soviets will bury the West, including America. Later he appeared at the United Nations and pounded his shoe loudly when he heard something he did not like. Krushchev threatened the then young President Kennedy to withdraw his order to stop Soviet naval ships attempting to enter Cuban waters during the Missile crisis. Krushchev lost his nerve and was the first to blink. However Krushchev did advocate peaceful coexistence with the West and negotiated with the US to reduce Cold War tensions. By 1964 his reforms had alienated powerful Soviet constituencies and conservatives led by Leonid Brezhnev ousted Khrushchev and he was permitted to retire to a country dacha where he died in 1971.[41]

Leonid Brezhnev

Leonid Brezhnev was born December 12, 1906 in Kamenskoe (now Dneprodzerzhinsk), Ukraine, son of a steel worker. He graduated from a technical college. majoring in engineering and metallurgy. He joined Komsomol in 1923 and the Communist party in 1931. He was drafted into the army and served as a political commissar in a tank factory. He held various technical and political posts. By the time Brezhnev joined the party, Stalin was in clear control. Since there were wide purges in the party and army during the 1930's many promotions opened to those who survived, including Brezhnev. Brezhnev was drafted and assigned to help relocate the industries

---

41 CNN Perspective Series, p. 1

of Dnepropetrovsk to Siberia and the East. The Germans invaded in June 1941.

He was made deputy head of political administration for the Southern Front and in 1942 when Ukraine was occupied by Germans, he was sent to the Caucasus. In 1943 he became head of the Political Department of the 18th Army. Thereafter he worked under Nikita Krushchev who became one of his important patrons. In 1946 he left the Red Army with the rank of Major General. He held several posts in Soviet Moldavia and then became a candidate member of the Presidium of the Communist Party. Brezhnev met Khrushchev in 1931 and become his protégé. After Stalin's death he was appointed to head one of the military positions in the Politburo. In 1956 he was recalled to Moscow from a post in Kazakhstan and assigned control of the defense industry, the space program, heavy industry and capital construction and was a senior member of Khrushchev's entourage. He backed Krushchev in a struggle with the Stalinist old guard and was rewarded as a full member of the Politburo. In October 1964 Brezhnev as Krushchev's successor, joined a group disenchanted by his increasingly erratic behavior and voted him out of office as Party First Secretary and Brezhnev was appointed to this post. Aleksei Kosygin was appointed Prime Minister and Mikoyan head of State, to be succeeded in 1965 by Nikolay Podgorny.

During the Krushchev years Brezhnev had supported Krushchev's denunciations of Stalin's arbitrary rule, the rehabilitation of many of the victims of Stalin's purges and the cautious liberalization of Soviet intellectual and cultural policy. But as soon as he became the leader Brezhnev began to reverse his positions and developed increasingly conservative and regressive attitudes. Under Yuri Andropov the KGB regained much of the power it had enjoyed under Stalin.

Brezhnev's first international crisis occurred in 1968 when the Communist leadership in Czechoslovakia under Alexander Dubcek tried to liberalize the Communist system (the Prague Spring). Brezhnev publicly criticized the Czech leadership as "revisionist" and "anti-Soviet." As First Secretary of the Czechoslovakian Communist Party Dubcek had tried without success to persuade Soviet leaders that they had no intention of removing Czechoslovakia from the Warsaw Pact, but simply wanted to democratize the government and loosen its association with the USSR. Dubcek had initiated a series of reforms that centered on increased expression, public debate, intellectual freedom and less press censorship. He wanted to create "Socialism with a Human Face." These reforms won mass support in Czechoslovakia, but the leaders of the USSR recognized that such a loosening of the ties was quite dangerous to continuing control of Warsaw Pact countries. Thus on August 20, 1968 Warsaw Pact forces (Soviet, East German, Polish, Hungarian and Bulgarian) troops occupied the country and Dubcek was replaced as head of the party by Gustav Husak. The invasion led to public protests by dissidents in the Soviet Union and his assertion that the Soviet Union had the right to interfere in the internal affairs of its satellites to "safeguard socialism" This became known as the Brezhnev Doctrine.

Under Brezhnev relations with China continued to deteriorate following the Sino-Soviet split which had broken out in the early 1960's. In 1969 Soviet and Chinese troops fought a series of clashes along their border on the

Ussuri River. Brezhnev also continued Soviet support for North Vietnam. Sino-American relations thawed beginning in 1971 as a result of President Nixon's secret trip to China to open US—Chinese relations . Nixon thereafter came to Moscow in 1972 and the two leaders signed the Strategic Arms Limitation Treaty (SALT I) marking the beginning of detente. (SALT II would be signed by Brezhnev and Jimmy Carter in 1979) The Paris Peace Accords of January 1973 officially ended the US involvement in the Vietnam War, removing a principal obstacle to improved Soviet-US relations.

In May Brezhnev visited West Germany and in June made a state visit to the US. The high point of détente was the signing of the Helsinki Final Act in 1975 which recognized the postwar frontiers of eastern and central Europe and in effect legitimized Soviet hegemony over the region. In return the Soviet Union agreed that participating States will respect human rights and fundamental freedoms, including the freedom of thought, conscience, religion or belief. There is to be no distinction because of race, sex, language or religion. However these undertakings were never honored and there was no apparent relaxation of tensions by the Soviet Union or its satellites. Also the issue of the right to emigrate for Soviet Jews became an increasing irritant in Soviet--US relations. The Summit in Vladivostok between President Gerald Ford and Brezhnev in November 1974 failed to resolve these issues.

The SALT I treaty effectively established parity in nuclear weapons between the US and Soviet Union. The Helsinki Treaty legitimated Soviet hegemony over eastern Europe and the US defeat in Vietnam. The Watergate scandal had weakened the prestige of the US. And for the first time the Soviet Union also became a global naval power. The USSR had extended its diplomatic and political influence in the Middle East and Africa and through Cuba had successfully intervened militarily in the 1975 civil war in Angola, and in the 1977-78 Ethiopia-Somalia War. In the meantime Brezhnev had forced the retirement of Podgorny and again assumed the position of Chairman of the Presidium of the Supreme Soviet.

During this period Brezhnev's health began to deteriorate and the economy of the USSR became stagnant. The economy was still heavily dependent on agriculture. Stalin's collectivization of agriculture had destroyed the independent peasantry and the farmers and workers were unable to keep up with rising demands for food made upon them. Likewise there were heavy demands placed on industry which could not be met. Similarly prestige projects like the space program and Baikal Amur Mainline (New Siberian rail line) imposed additional production demands which could not be met. Public housing and the state health and education systems also stagnated, reducing morale and productivity.

The response was a huge underground or black market economy which became necessary to meet the demands of those who could pay. This problem along with corruption among regional officials decreased Brezhnev's popular support. Several high regional officials were put on trial when Yuri Andropov succeeded Brezhnev. Brezhnev's last years were marked by declining health, increasing frailty and by a growing personality cult. He received and was flattered by many medals showing his accomplishments, real or not.

In December, 1979 Brezhnev and his inner circle made an ill fated decision to invade Afghanistan in support of a struggling Communist regime. This action led to a sudden end to détente and the imposition of a US grain embargo. In March 1982 Brezhnev suffered a stroke and thereafter struggled to retain control and died of a heart attack on November 10, 1982. He was honored with a large and impressive funeral.

Yuri Vladimirovich Andropov

Yuri Vladimirovich Andropov was born on June 15, 1914 and joined the Communist Youth League (Komsomol) in 1930. And benefiting from vacancies created by Stalin's purges, he rose rapidly in the ranks becoming First Secretary of the new Yaroslov Komsomol Central Committee of the Karelo-Finnish Republic (1940-1944). He participated in partisan guerrilla activities and then was transferred to Moscow in 1951. After Stalin's death in 1953 he was transferred to Budapest where he served as an Embassy counselor and then became ambassador to Hungary in 1954. He sent a steady stream of reports to Moscow which resulted in the decision to invade Hungary in 1956.

He was appointed head of the KGB in 1967. Dissent was severely repressed and dissidents frequently confined to psychiatric hospitals. Andropov became a full member of the Politburo in 1973 and Communist party general secretary a short time after Brezhnev's death on November 10, 1982. During his short tenure (15 months), the USSR was still at war in Afghanistan and he tried to persuade the Europeans not to allow the US to station Pershing missiles in Germany and tried to improve the efficiency of the Soviet economy. It was on his watch that Soviet forces shot down a South Korean civilian air liner, killing all 269 aboard. Andropov died on February 9, 1984 of acute kidney failure.

Konstantin Ustinovich Chernenko

Konstantin Chernenko was born September 24, 1911 in Krasnoyarsk, Siberia and died on March 10, 1984. He was the son of a poor Siberian farmer. Chernenko's career was basicly that of a clerk of the Communist party. He also served as a border guard. He left no legacy or memoirs. He was chosen as General Secretary of the party on Andropov's death, and at that time was 72 years of age and suffered from chronic emphysema. During the second world war he served as a clerk in Siberia in charge of agitprop. During the 1930s and 1940s he was a party bureaucrat in charge of propaganda, literature and other party duties in Krasnoyarsk. He would have spent his life in Siberia had he not met Leonid Brezhnev in Moldova.

When Brezhnev went to Moscow in 1956 he brought Chernenko along as his chief of staff. In 1966 he became a member of the Central Committee and in 1978 a full member of the Politburo. When Brezhnev died in November, 1982, Chernenko decided to support Andropov for the position of General Secretary. Because of Andropov's deteriorating health Chernenko was soon chairing Politburo meetings in his place. Despite his doctor's warning that he was too sick for the job, Chernenko was elected General Secretary on Andropov's death. His health however rapidly deteriorated and the running of the country was basicly left to Mikhail Gorbachev. By the end of 1984 Chernenko could hardly leave the hospital and the Politburo was affixing a facsimile of his signature to all letters.

Mikhail Sergeyevich Gorbachev

Mikhail S. Gorbachev was born on March 2, 1931 in Stavropol near the Caucasus Mountains[42]. He was the last General Secretary of the Communist Party of the Soviet Union,(CPSU) serving from 1985 until 1991 and the last head of state of the USSR, serving from 1988 until its collapse in 1991. His attempts at reform (perestroika and glasnost) and his summit meetings with President Regan helped end the Cold War, but also led to the dissolution of the Soviet Union, and in 1990 won him the Nobel Peace prize. He is presently the leader of the Union of Social Democrats, a political party founded on October 20, 2007.

Growing up, Gorbachev worked as a farm laborer and machinery operator. His grandfather had spent 9 years in the gulag for withholding grain from the collective's harvest. However despite the hardships, he did very well in the fields and in the classroom. He was one of the best students in his class and excelled in history and mathematics. He helped his father harvest a record crop and received an award for this service at age 16. Beginning in 1950, Gorbachev studied law at the University of Moscow.

By 1985 Gorbachev had worked his way up the ranks to the Politburo. He had been especially helpful to Andropov and later Chernenko when they were both sick. He joined the Communist Party while at the Univer-

---

[42] The underlying facts and events can be found in wikipedia.org.

DEMOCRACY TODAY IN RUSSIA

sity and also met his wife Raisa a fellow student. They were married in September, 1953. Upon his graduation from college they moved back to Stavropol where he immersed himself in party work, joining Komsomol and serving energetically as First Secretary of the Stavropol City Committee. He was then promoted to the regional and higher agricultural committees until he reached the politburo.[43] In the meantime Raisa had given birth to two daughers and they were busy with family life.

When Andropov and then Chernenko fell sick, Gorbachev took over many of their tasks and when Chernenko died in 1985 Gorbachev was quickly proposed by Andrei Gromyko, the long term (28 years) Foreign Minister to be General Secretary of the party. His principal potential opponent (Grishin) fortuitously was traveling in San Francisco at the time Chernenko died and those supporting the candidacy of Gorbachev rushed through the preliminaries, and completed the appointment before Grishin could mount an effective counter campaign. Gromyko was promoted to President and he was replaced as Foreign Minister by Eduard Shevardnadze of Georgia who shared Gorbachev's philosophy. Since Gorbachev had been doing much of the work of the Politburo already he was fully prepared to take control as soon as he was elected. That same year (1985) he announced that the Soviet economy was stalled and that reorganization was needed in the form of perestroika[44] and glasnost. Gor-

---

43 Gorbachev also received a degree from the Stavropol Agricultural Institute in 1967.
44 In 1988 the Law on Cooperatives was enacted. This was a radical economic reform which permitted private ownership of businesses in the service, manufacturing and foreign trade sectors.

bachev introduced many radical reforms including liberalizing the press and speech. He wrote and released his book "Perestroika: New Thinking for our Country and the World" which outlined his main ideas for reform.

Gorbachev took advantage of poor oversight of programs by key Soviet officers to get new blood into the system. For example when a young West German, Mathias Rust managed to embarrass the military by flying a small plan into Moscow and landing in Red Square, Gorbachev made sweeping personnel changes in the military beginning at the top, appointing Dmitry Yazov as the new Minister of Defense. In 1987 he rehabilitated many opponents of Stalin. In 1988 Gorbachev introduced glasnost, a radical change, which abandoned detailed oversight of speech in the USSR.

He acknowledged that his liberalizing policies of glasnost and perestroika owed much to Alexander Dubcek's "Socialism with a human face." Elections to the Congress of People's Deputies were held in March and April 1989, the first free elections since 1917. Yeltsin was elected in Moscow and became an increasingly vocal critic of Gorbachev.

In 1989 there was a dramatic collapse of the Eastern Block and the withdrawal from Afghanistan. On November 9, 1989 the people in the German Democratic Republic (GDR) broke down the Berlin Wall following a peaceful protest. Gorbachev decided not to interfere with the processes in Germany and stated that German reunification was an internal German matter. Gorbachev was hailed in the West for his 'New Thinking' in foreign affairs. He sought to improve relations and trade with the West by reducing Cold War tensions. In 1985 he announced the suspension of the deployment of SS-20s in Europe and the beginning of a close personal relationship with President Ronald Reagan and other Western leaders. In 1986 he proposed elimination of intermediate range nuclear weapons in Europe and a strategy for eliminating all nuclear weapons by the year 2000.

In October, 1986 Gorbachev and Reagan met in Reykjavik, Icelend to discuss reducing intermediate range nuclear weapons in Europe. In February 1988 Gorbachev had announced the full withdrawal of Soviet forces from Afghanistan. [45]. Also in 1988 Gorbachev announced abandonment of the Brezhnev Doctrine and that Eastern block nations would be allowed to freely determine their own internal affairs. This abandonment led to a string of revolutions in Eastern Europe in which Communism collapsed. The loosening of Soviet hegemony over Eastern Europe effectively ended the Cold War. For this accomplishment Gorbachev received the Nobel Peace Prize on October 15, 1990.

While Gorbachev's political initiatives of freedom and democracy were positive for the USSR and its allies, the economic policies brought the country close to disaster. Severe shortages in basic food supplies led to wartime distribution restrictions. Also democratization undermined the power of the CPSU and Gorbachev himself. The giving up of censorship and attempts to create more political openness had the effect of reawakening long suppressed nationalist and anti Russian feelings in the republics, especially in the Baltics (Lithuania, Latvia and Estonia) and in nationalist feelings in Georgia,

---

[45] It is estimated that 28,000 Soviet troops were killed in that conflict between 1979 and 1989.

Ukraine, Armenia and Azerbaijan. Nationalist turmoil began in January 1990. There were riots in Azerbaijan, Moldavia and Armenia.

On March 15, 1990 Gorbachev was elected President of the Soviet Union by the Congress of People's Deputies. During all this period because of glasnost[46], embarrassing facts continued to emerge from history, including discovery of the secret agreements between Stalin and Hitler contemplating annexation of the Baltic Republics by the USSR and that the NKVD had carried out the infamous Katyn Massacre of Polish army officers during World War II for which Nazi Germany had been blamed.

In the meantime Boris Yeltsin had been elected Chairman of the Presidium of the Russian SFSR, making him leader of the Russian Federation. Also the federation Republics were declaring their laws to be superior to those of the USSR. Gorbachev was being granted powers to rule by decree and Eduard Shevardnadze fearful of an impending dictatorship, resigned in protest. Gorbachev's efforts during the next months were consumed by attempts to find a political solution to the Baltic countries threats to break away as well as accommodating nationalities which wanted to form autonomous republics.

Hardliners were completely opposed to any solution which might lead to a break up of the Soviet Union, and on the eve of signing the new voluntary treaty, the hardliners struck. The self-named 'State Emergency Committee' launched the August coup in 1991 in an attempt to remove Gorbachev from power and to prevent the sign-

---

46 Gorbachev's goal in undertaking glasnost was to pressure conservatives within the Party who opposed his policies of economic restructuring.

ing of the proposed new union treaty.[47] During this time Gorbachev spent 3 days, (19-21) in August under house arrest at his dacha in the Crimea. Political support in the meantime had swung to Yeltsin, whose defiance had led to the collapse of the coup. In several humiliating acts Gorbachev was publicly forced to fire large numbers of his Politburo, party and other officials. Some were arrested for high treason including Kryuchkov, Yazov, Pavlov and Yanayev. Pugachev was shot and Akhromeyev was found hanging in his Kremlin office.

After the coup many of the republics declared their independence. Yeltsin ordered the CPSU to suspend its activities on the territory of Russia. Gorbachev resigned as General Secretary of the CPSU and advised the Central Committee to dissolve. On December 1 Ukraine voted for independence and on December 8 the presidents of Russia, Ukraine and Belarus met to found the Commonwealth of Independent States. Gorbachev agreed with Yeltsin on December 17 to dissolve the Soviet Union. He resigned on December 25 and the Soviet Union was formally dissolved the next day.

Boris Nikolayevich Yeltsin

Boris Yeltsin was born in Sverdlovsk (Ekaterinburg), Russia on February 1 1931[48]. His father was a construction worker and his mother a seamstress. He was good

---

47 For Gorbachev's account of the coup see his book, Mikhail Gorbachev, The August Coup, the Truth and the Lessons. Harper Collins, 1991.
48 The basic underlying facts of Yeltsin's life can be found in Wikipedia.org and Yeltsin's Autobiography, Against the Grain, Summit Books, 1990; and Boris Yeltsin from Bolshevik to Democrat, John Morrison, A Dutton Book 1991.

at most sports and attended the Urals State Technical University in Sverdlovsk majoring in construction. Upon graduation in 1955, he worked as a construction supervisor, and was promoted quickly through the ranks of construction responsibilities. He joined the Communist Party of the Soviet Union (CPSU) nomenklatura in 1968 and by 1977 he was party boss in Sverdlovsk. He met and impressed Gorbachev and was soon appointed Mayor of Moscow (First Secretary of the CPSU Moscow City Committee) where he served from December 24 1985 to 1987. Yeltsin was sacked following a confrontation with Yegor Ligachev and Gorbachev concerning Gorbachev's wife Raisa meddling in affairs of state. In 1987 at a meeting of the CPSU, he lashed out at the Politburo, expressing discontent at the pace of reform and the servility shown to the General Secretary. He then asked to resign from the Politburo. He was demoted and fired from the post of first secretary of the Moscow City Committee.

Attempts were made to smear him for drunkenness and bad behavior. However these attacks added to his popularity. In March 1989 he was elected to the Congress of People's Deputies as the Moscow district delegate. In May 1990 he was elected chairman of the Presidium of the Supreme Soviet of the Russian SFSR. In June 1991 Yeltsin won 57% of the popular vote in the democratic presidential elections defeating Gorbachev's preferred candidate Nikolai Ryzhkov. On August 18, 1991 a coup against Gorbachev was launched by Vladimir Kryuchkov and other party members opposed to perestroika. Gorbachev was held at his dacha in the Crimea while Yeltsin raced to the Moscow White House (residence of the RSFSR Supreme Soviet) to challenge the coup.

DEMOCRACY TODAY IN RUSSIA

Although the White House was surrounded by military forces, the troops defected in the face of mass popular demonstrations and refused to support the coup. The coup collapsed following Yeltsin's fiery speech from the top of a tank. Gorbachev was rescued and returned to Moscow.

Gorbachev's powers however were fatally compromised and the principal power structures in the meantime had swung to Yeltsin. In the fall of 1991 the Russian government took over the union government ministry by ministry. On November 6, 1991, Yeltsin issued a decree banning Communist Party activities though out the RSFSR. In December, 1991 Ukraine voted for independence from the USSR, and Yeltsin met with the leaders of Ukraine and Belarus to announce the dissolution of the Soviet Union and the formation of a voluntary Commonwealth of Independent States (CIS). On December 24 the Russian Federation took the Soviet Union's seat in the United Nations and next day Gorbachev resigned and the USSR ceased to exist.

Yeltsin resolved to embark on a program of radical economic reform with the goal of restructuring Russia's economic system by converting it to a free market. In 1991 Yeltsin sought advice from Western economists such as the IMF, the World Bank and US Treasury which had developed standard recipes for transition economies. Yegor Gaidar, a 35 year old Russian economist became Yeltsin's deputy for conversion and he favored a shock therapy transformation.

In January, 1992 Yeltsin ordered liberalization of foreign trade, prices and currency, and at the same time a policy of macro economic stabilization. The stabilization would be achieved by imposing a harsh austerity regime designed to control inflation. Under Yeltsin's program interest rates were raised to very high levels to restrict credit and to bring state spending and revenues into balance. Yeltsin also imposed heavy new taxes, reduced government subsidies and made steep cuts in state welfare spending. These strong actions shut down many industries and brought about a depression. The reforms also devastated living standards. During the 1990s Russia's GDP fell by 50 per cent, unemployment grew dramatically and incomes fell. Hyperinflation caused by the Central Bank of Russia's loose monetary policy wiped out many personal savings accounts and millions of Russians were plunged into poverty.

Throughout 1992 and 1993 Yeltsin battled the Supreme Soviet and Congress of People's Deputies for control over the government. During 1992 the speaker of the Supreme Soviet Ruslan Khasbulatov challenged Yeltsin's reforms and the Congress turned down his proposed candidate for prime minister Yegor Gaidar. Eventually a compromise candidate was installed, but escalating the conflict, Yeltsin announced in a televised address on March 20, 1993 that he was going to assume special powers to implement his reform program. In response the Congress tried but failed to remove Yeltsin from office through impeachment. In September 1993 Yeltsin announced that he was going to disband the Congress of People's Deputies and Supreme Soviet. He intended to rule by decree until a new parliament was elected and a referendum on a new constitution was completed. In the meantime the Supreme Soviet declared Yeltsin removed from office as president and Vice President Alexander

Rutskoy was sworn in as acting President. Thousands of supporters of the parliament took to the streets in support of anti-Yeltsin demonstrators. They protested terrible living conditions under Yeltsin. The GDP had declined by half; corruption was rampant, violent crime was skyrocketing, medical services were collapsing, food and fuel were increasingly scarce and Yeltsin was being blamed for it all. However in a massive show of force Yeltsin called up tanks to shell the Russian White House, Russia's parliament building and blasted out his opponents who were holed up inside. Thousands were wounded and hundreds died.

The Supreme Soviet was dissolved in December 1993 elections to be replaced by the newly established parliament the State Duma. In the election Yeltsin's economic supporters were overwhelmed. The referendum held at the same time approved the new constitution which significantly expanded the powers of the president, giving Yeltsin a right to appoint the members of the government, to dismiss the prime minister and in some cases dissolve the Duma.

On December 12 1994 Yeltsin ordered the military invasion of Chechnya. This action lasted for two years. Under a 1996 Peace Accord granting Chechnya greater autonomy, federal forces were withdrawn from a devastated Chechnya.

Following collapse of the Soviet Union, Yeltsin promoted privatization as a means of spreading ownership of shares in former state enterprises as widely as possible. In the early 1990s Anatoly Chubais, Yeltsin's deputy for economic policy was the leading privatization advocate in Russia. In late 1992 Yeltsin launched a program of free vouchers to jump start the program. All Russian citizens were issued vouchers for purchase of shares in selected state enterprises. Soon after issuance, the vouchers ended up in the hands of intermediaries who would pay immediate cash for them. By 1995 Yeltsin was struggling to finance Russia's growing foreign debt and he therefore initiated a new form of privatization in which the government exchanged shares in some of the most valuable state enterprises in exchange for bank loans. However the deals were essentially giveaways of valuable state assets to a small group of tycoons in finance, industry, energy, telecommunications and the media who came to be known as the oligarchs. By early 1996 substantial ownership of shares of major firms were acquired at low prices by a small group of people. These included Boris Berezovsky who controlled several banks and national media and became one of Yeltsin's principal backers. This group also included Mikhail Khodorkovsky, Vladimir Potanin, Vladimir Bogdanov, Rem Viakhirev, Vagigit Alekperov, Alexander Smolensky, Victor Vekselberg, Mikhail Friedman and Roman Abramovich.

Although polls showed Yeltsin's popularity at near zero, he decided to run for president anyway in the 1996 elections and engaged his privatization chief Chubais as his campaign manager. In the spring of 1996 Chubais and Yeltsin recruited a team of financial and media oligarchs to finance the presidential campaign. In return Chubais permitted certain Russian business leaders to acquire majority stakes in some of Russia's most valuable state owned assets. Yeltsin campaigned energetically and promised to give up some of his more unpopular economic reforms, boost welfare spending, end the war in Chechnya and pay wage and pension arrears. Gennady Zyuganov, the Communist Party candidate lacked Yeltsin's financial backing and when all the votes were counted Yeltsin had won 53.8% of the vote compared with 40.3% for Zyuganov.

Yeltsin was unable to keep his campaign promises except for ending the Chechen war. Later in 1996 Yeltsin underwent quintuple heart bypass surgery and stayed in the hospital for months. In the meantime he continued to suffer from chronic alchoholism and a neurological disorder which affected his balance. The world press followed his health closely and there was a fear he might die in office.

In 1998 a political and economic crisis emerged when the government defaulted on its debts, causing financial markets to panic and the ruble to collapse. In 1999 Yeltsin survived another impeachment attempt. On August 9, 1999 he fired his prime minister Sergei Stepashin and for the fourth time fired his entire cabinet. Yeltsin appointed Vladimir Putin, relatively unknown at that time, to replace Stepashin. On December 31, 1999 he announced that he had resigned and that Putin had taken his place as acting president with elections due to take place on March 26, 2000.

Yeltsin kept a low profile after his resignation. Following the Beslan school hostage crisis and near concurrent terrorist attacks in Moscow, Putin launched an initiative to replace elections of regional governors with a system whereby they would be appointed by the president and approved by regional legislatures. Yeltsin and Gorbachev publicly criticized Putin's plan as a step away from democracy. But on Yeltsin's death on April 23 2007, Putin lauded him for his role in bringing democracy to Russia.

Shopping in Moscow

Moscow meat market

Local Moscow band entertaining passersby

Children enjoying their play time

Who started the South Ossetia, Georgia war.

In August, 2008 Georgia and Russia engaged in a brief shooting war over South Ossetia. Each country accused the other of starting the war. Following intense pressure brought on each of the parties by the United States the UN and European Union among others, the belligerent parties stopped their shooting and withdrew their armed forces. At first it would seem that the fight was over a tempest in a teapot, but much is at stake and it would be helpful to examine the geographical, political and economic factors which lead up to this mini-war.

On August 14, 2008 US Defense Secretary Robert Gates ruled out US military force in Georgia but warned Russia of long term damage to its relations with Washington if it does not pull back its forces. "If Russia does not step back from its aggressive posture and actions in Georgia, the US-Russian relationship could be adversely affected for years to come." Gates said it appeared the Russians seized an opportunity to punish Georgia, not just for its actions in the enclaves but for its pro-US policies. "I think that the Russians' further message was to all of the parts of the former Soviet Union as a signal about trying to integrate with the West and move outside of the longtime Russian sphere of influence."

President Medvedev of Russia described his feelings in dealing with the Georgians and his reactions. This was one of the worst days of my life."I'll never forget that night." I was on vacation and was told about the invasion at one in the morning. I had several long telephone conversations with President Bush and described Saakashvili as a man we (Russia) will not do business with. He's an unpredictable pathological and mentally unstable drug abuser.: Mikheil Saakashvili is the President of Georgia and was elected to replace Eduard Shevardnadze. He was born December 21, 1967. He took office January 25, 2004. His wife is Dutch. He speaks fluent English, French, Russian and Ukrainian. His mother is a historian and his father a doctor. He graduated from the International University in Kiev and received an LLM from Columbia Law School He also had studied at George Washington University and in Strasbourg. He worked in New York with a law firm there.

Saakashvili had worked for Shevardnadze as Minister of Justice, but then quit, protesting corruption and then formed his own party and was elected President. He is strongly pro Western, and is seeking membership in NATO. He has good relations with the US, complicated however by his volatile behavior. He is described as difficult to manage and is criticized for his risky moves catching the US unprepared .

Ossetia is a small area containing a population of about 100,000 which spans portions of the Caucasus mountains to the north and another portion to the south. The northern portion is a part of Russia and the southern portion has been historically part of Georgia. The Ossetians were originally descendent from the Alans which in turn were related to Iranians and others. They became Christians during the early Middle Ages. They fell under Mongol rule and were pushed out of their homeland south of the Don River. Part of their group migrated over the Caucuses mountains to Georgia where they became what is now known as South Ossetians. The northern group became known as North Ossetians and came under Russian control about 1767. Most Ossetians (61%) became Christian; but a significant number became Muslim. Modern South Ossetia was annexed to Russia in 1801, along with Georgia, and was absorbed into the Russian Empire. Thereafter there were a series of Ossetian rebellions during which various claims of independence were made.

At the time of the Communist revolution, the Menshevik Georgian government accused Ossetians of cooperating with the Bolsheviks. A Soviet Georgian government was established by the Red Army in 1921. and the South Ossetian Autonomous Oblast was created in April 1922. Ossetians had their own language. Under the rule of the Georgian government during Soviet times, Ossetia had some degree of autonomy including speaking and teaching the Ossetian language in school.

Nationalism began to arise in 1989 and in November the South Ossetian Regional Council asked the Georgian Supreme Council to upgrade it to an autonomous republic. When the Georgian council refused the upgrade, the Ossetians proclaimed themselves a Soviet Democratic Republic, fully sovereign within the USSR. Georgia counter attacked by abolishing South Ossetia's autonomous status. Violence broke out at the end of 1991. Many Southern villages were attacked and burned as well as Georgian houses and schools in Tskhinvali, capital of South Ossetia. About 1,000 died and 100,000 ethnic Ossetians fled, mainly to North Ossetia Other Ossetians were resettled in the north in uninhabited areas from which Stalin had expelled Ingush people in 1944. One of the bloodiest recent episodes of which most observers were aware was the terrorist hostage incident at the Beslan school in which 335 civilians, mostly children were killed.

The boundary disputes of South and North Ossetia, although they may not appear large, must be peacefully settled since new members cannot be accepted into NATO unless all boundary disputes have been resolved. Also unsettled boundary disputes could serve as flash points for future wars particularly in the former USSR which has many bits and pieces of land which can be contested. Russia was a colonial power, but its colonies were mostly contiguous. If Russia is successful in threatening or pressuring its neighbors in its reacquisition of former colonies, this could weaken the will to resist Russia's efforts on the part of such former colonies as Ukraine, Estonia, Latvia and Lithuania to give up their territories under threats from Moscow. Moscow could and would contend that all the questions related to the independence and territorial conflicts of Georgia, Armenia, Azerbaijan, are Soviet internal affairs.

In 1992 Georgia was forced to accept a ceasefire with Russia. Under the cease fire, the government of Georgia and South Ossetian separatists pledged not to use force against one another and Georgia agreed not to impose sanctions against South Ossetia. A peacekeeping force of Ossetians, Russians and Georgians was established. Also the Organization for Security and Cooperation in Europe (OSCE) created a mission to monitor peacekeeping. There was general peace until 2004 when in June, 2004 Georgia strengthened its efforts to control smuggling in the area. Because of inadequate government control in South Ossetia, hostage taking, shootouts and bombing left dozens dead and wounded. Also Georgia objected to increasing Russian economic and political presence, considered the peacekeeping non neutral and demanded its replacement. The parties were sliding toward a war status since these conditions required by Georgia were not met.

On August 4, 2008 five battalions of the Russian 58th Army were moved to the vicinity of the Roki Tunnel, which passes through the Caucuses Mountains and connects north and south Ossetia. Violent conflict began with clashes occurring on August 6, 2008. Each side claimed that the other had violated the cease fire. On August 8, 2008 the same day as the Summer Olympics were opened in Beijing, China, Georgian forces were ordered to move into and control Tskhinvali "to restore constitutional order in the entire region." Within hours Russian troops also moved into South Ossetia as part of a "peace enforcement" operation pushing the Georgian army out of South Ossetia and moving into Georgia proper by occupying Gori (birthplace of Stalin), Kareli and other cities.

At the same time Russian forces entered another breakaway region of Abkhazia, occupying the Black Sea port of Poti. On August 8, 2008 Georgian troops and armor rolled into South Ossetia and shelled Tskhinvale and reported that three Russian Su-24 aircraft had intruded on Georgian airspace. The same day 12 Russian peacekeepers were killed and about 150 injured.

Russian prime minister Putin condemned the aggressive actions by Georgian troops and stated that Russia would be compelled to retaliate.[49] Georgia attempted to remove South Ossetia forces from Tskhinvali on August

---

49 Putin accused the Western press of an "immoral and dishonest account of what happened." He said Russia had no choice but to intervene following what he alleged was Georgian aggression.. Mr. Putin also accused the US of behaving like the Roman Empire by believing it could pursue its own interests and extending its influence to the Caucasus without regard for Russia's point of view…"God forbid that we should tread on US toes in its backyard."…he insisted that current tensions did not amount to the start of a new Cold War and that Russia might suffer diplomatic or economic isolation because of the crisis. But Russia was prepared to work with Western partners and wanted a constructive relationship with the European Union… But Russia should be treated as an equal partner and all sides agree on new common rules of behavior based on international law See BBC News 9/11/2008

DEMOCRACY TODAY IN RUSSIA

8. The next day Russia deployed its forces and targeted Georgian military infrastructure. Russia and Georgia then negotiated a cease fire and pulled back most of their respective forces. (Wikipedia, South Ossetia)

The Russian parliament voted in favor of recognizing the independence of South Ossetia and Abkhazia[50]. Western Powers condemned Russia's unilateral recognition[51] due to the violation of Georgia's territorial integrity.[52] Russia then offered residents the choice of accepting Russian citizenship or leaving.[53] Former US envoy Richard Holbooke said the conflict could encourage separatist movements in other former Soviet states along Russia's western border[54]. These former states which could fall prey to Moscow's threats could include Ukraine[55], Lithuania, Estonia and Latvia, among others.

---

50 Russian president Dmitri Medvedev defied US pressure and signed a decree recognizing the independence of the breakaway Georgian territories of South Ossetia and Abkhazia. NPR 8/28/2008
51 Russia Today: News, 8/29/2008
52 Ibid.
53 Putin has declared that Russia will not be isolated because it protected its citizens and fulfilled its peacekeeping missions Russia Today: News 8/29/2008
54 The Bush administration has accused Russia of trying to reassert its sphere of influence and says the US will not tolerate it. Russia, in turn, has accused the US of arming and whitewashing what it calls a "criminal regime" in Georgia. NPR 8/28/2008
55 The president of Ukraine, Viktor Yushchenko takes the Russian threats quite seriously, particularly following Russia's sudden price increase of gas and oil supplies last year. He has denounced as a traitor Ukraine's prime minister Yulia Tymoshenko for not denouncing the recent Russian invasion of Georgia. Russia is doing everything it can to keep Ukraine and Georgia out of

The Republic of South Ossetia consists of a checkerboard of Georgian and Ossetian inhabited towns and villages in close proximity to one another and being administered by Georgia or South Ossetia, essentially by whichever group was in the majority. This proximity brought about a dangerous situation as to whose orders should be followed.

Evidence has been produced by US and Georgian journalists that the South Ossetia—Georgian war was planned well in advance by both Russia[56] and Georgia, with each attempting to blame the other as the aggressor. South Ossetia has been coveted by both historically. Russia had been assigned the duty of keeping the peace following the split in 1991 of the break away provinces of Ossetia and Abkhasia on the Black Sea. Evidence shows that Russia attempted to provoke Georgia into attacking and then blaming the first move on Georgia.

Each year Russia would conduct "peace keeping" exercises in Ossetia. During the spring of 2008 the Russian Federal Security Bureau and the local KGB organized a series of Russian provocations in Abkhasia and South Ossetia. The aim was to draw Georgia into armed conflict. Railway Troops began preparations at the end of May. During this period and into early summer rail wagons could not be requisitioned for normal export of goods. The rail wagons were reserved for the Caucasus since

---

NATO.
56 See Facts and Arts, 9/21/2008

they would be needed for the transport of heavy military equipment.

The war exercise Caucasus 2008 started in July near the coming war zone. Officially 8000 troops were to be involved. The first concrete threats of war against Georgia were made at the end of April. According to one of the commanding generals the "peace enforcement operations" could include "actions in view of a possible escalation of the conflict situation in South Ossetia and Abkhazia." At the same time a concentrated cyber attack was begun against the websites of the President and the Government of Georgia, swamping them with spam and hacking. The Caucuses 2008 exercise was concluded on August 2 and by then provocations against Georgia had increased dramatically. On August 3 South Ossetia had given the order to start evacuating the population in the risk zone to Russia where refugee camps already stood ready and waiting. Many Russian journalists began streaming into South Ossetia.

Georgia released two intercepted phone messages originally published by the New York Times purporting to show that Russia, not Georgia initiated the war[57]. These calls, assuming their authenticity, show that Russian tanks and troops entered South Ossetia many hours before Georgia began its offensive against separatist forces. The releases were made on the authority of Mikhail Saakashvili, the young president of Georgia. He said he tried to ease tensions with a unilateral cease fire, but the Russian leaders had already decided to invade. The phone

---

57   See SF Chronicle, p. 11, Sept 17, 2008.

calls are between a South Ossetian border guard at the southern mouth of the Roki tunnel and another guard at Tskhinvali, the headquarters in the regional capital. The first call was made at 3:41 a.m. on August 7 stating "they have moved armored personnel carriers out and the tunnel is full." The next call was about 10 minutes later saying that "armor and people" had emerged from the tunnel about 20 minutes earlier.

The Russian Foreign Ministry dismissed the claims of the telephone interception as "not serious." Before the war Russia had 500 peacekeeping troops in South Ossetia so that their mere presence is not damning. Saakashvili, whose nation is seeking NATO membership, angrily rejected Russian suggestions that the forces in the tunnel were part of the peacekeeping rotation. NATO's Secretary General Jaap de Hoop Scheffer speaking in Tbilisi confirmed that when Georgia completes various steps, including making democratic progress, it will be offered NATO membership. "Despite the difficult situation, we expect Georgia to firmly stay the course of democracy and reform." "Russia's use of force was disproportionate and Russia must now comply with all elements of the six-point plan." The Secretary General said that NATO will meet for a summit in December, but did not say whether Georgia would be given a Membership Action Plan (a roadmap for accession).[58]

[59]Russian spokesmen contended that Russia did not expect that Georgia would attack. Prime Minister Pu-

---
58 See BBC News.
59 See BBC News. 1, 9/15/2008 (International Herald Tribune 9/16/2008, p.1)

tin was at the Olympics in Beijing, President Medvedev was on a cruise on the Volga River and the Minister of Defense was at the Black Sea on vacation. According to the Russians, the war began at 11:30 PM, August 7 when President Saakashvili of Georgia ordered an attack on Russian positions in Tshkinvali and Russian combat forces crossed the border into South Ossetia only later.

Frictions between Georgia and South Ossetia which has declared de facto independence, have simmered for years, but intensified when Mr. Saakashvili came to power in Georgia and made national unification a centerpiece of his agenda. Saakashvili is loathed by the Kremlin, partly because he has positioned himself as a spokesman for democracy movements and alignment with the West.[60] Earlier in the year Russia announced that it was expanding support for the separatist regions and Georgia labeled this an act of annexation. In the early 1990's South Ossetia and Abkhazia gained de facto independence from Georgia after the Soviet Union collapsed. There was tenuous peace monitored by Russian peacekeepers but frictions with Georgia increased sharply in 2004 when Saakashvili was elected president.

Russia's military offensive and contentions with respect to Georgia are not consistent with United Nations actions it had previously agreed to. In April, 2008 Russia approved UN Security Council resolution 1808 ratifying Georgia's sovereignty, independence and territorial integrity. Russia however appeals to its constitutional "right" to defend the "life and dignity" of all Russian

---

60 New York Times. Com 8/9/2008

citizens regardless of where they live. It has also declared its right to a sphere of interest that includes "especially, but not exclusively, neighbouring states." Russia sees it as a threat to its interests that others establish relationships with the countries in its sphere of interest. This has become known as the Putin doctrine. Putin was disappointed with both the disintegration of the Soviet Union and the way in which the West, especially the US have acted in the world and humiliated Russia by their nonchalant treatment.

The campaign against Georgia came after a throughgoing risk analysis. At the very heart of Putin's aggressive nationalism is his firm belief that the power of the West is on the wane.[61] And as a part of the risk analysis, Russia plans to provide military aid to South Ossetia and Abkhazia and it also takes into account that there will be continued risk to the operation of the Baku-Tbilisi-Ceyhand oil pipeline. Russia has coveted control over the oil and gas pipelines which run through Georgia to Turkey. It also seeks control of the flow of oil and gas through Georgia to Armenia, and to Turkey and the Black Sea and Mediterranian as well as controlling the flow through Ukraine. With these routes, it would have a near monopoly of the oil and gas flows into Europe. Russia has already demonstrated to Ukraine that if it does not meet its terms and conditions of fuel delivery it can cut off the fuel entirely and on short notice. This control can also be used to limit flows at reasonable prices to Iran and Georgia. Thus

---

61   Facts and Arts, Sept 12, 2008

Russia could cut off Iran's land route for the delivery of goods if the Strait of Hormuz were blocked.[62]

The disputes and arguments between Russia and Georgia can easily escalate into a more serious conflict since substantial oil and money are involved in the outcome. Also the fact that Russia is now seeking to loosen the ties that bind Russia and its former colonies make this dispute a model for anticipating future conflict with Russia.

---

62 Howard Schweber, Russia, Georgia and Iran

CONCLUSION

Since the collapse of the Soviet Union in 1991 Russia and its present and former colonies have followed a chaotic path seeking to transform a communist dictatorship into a democracy. And this path has proved to be difficult. During the most democratic period under the command of Boris Yeltsin there was much corruption and political stress. While there is still much corruption there is less political stress and hence less democracy. The economy was transformed from a command economy where prices and allocation of goods and services would be fixed by party specialists to a free market economy. During this chaotic period Russian citizens learned very little about democracy except that it meant shortages or absence of goods and services; it meant resort to the black market if they wanted to participate in getting some share of goods. And it meant high crime rates.

Democracy meant constant chaos, and bribery for meaningful participation in the economy. Since the year 2000 when Vladimir Putin was appointed acting president by Boris Yeltsin, he took immediate control to attempt to solve the problems plaguing Russian society. His moves were not all democratic, but judging from public perceptions, Putin has earned the respect of 81% of the electorate. Putin groomed his chief deputy Dmitri Medvedev to take his place as president. Putin would like to continue acting as President and has worked out an arrangement with Medvedev whereby Putin has been appointed his prime minister for the time being. A constitutional amendment has now been approved by the Russian Duma allowing a presidential term of six, rather than four years and so it is likely that in the not too distant future Medvedev will resign the presidency and Putin will take his place.

In this brief book I have identified and discussed the major problems and solutions Putin and Medvedev have been facing and their attempts to bring about democracy; and in the words of Putin to bring about a modern and prosperous state. Since Putin will be bound by the historical hand he is dealt, I have discussed briefly the evolution of democracy and capitalism, and the Russian burdens since the time of Stalin to the present

Printed in the United States
143784LV00001B/20/P